Musings

Suhasini Ramakrishnan

Musings

PARTRIDGE

To order additional copies of this book, contact
Partridge India
000 800 10062 62
orders.india@partridgepublishing.com

www.partridgepublishing.com/india

Contents

Dedication

This book is my first ever attempt to publish my poetry and also my first attempt at finding a bearing for myself in this literary ocean of people gifted with the ability to make prose and poetry sound magical.

This book is a dedication to my mother Prabha and my brother Arun.

Thank you for standing by me, bearing with my idiosyncrasies, reading my rough drafts, giving me space when I needed it and knowing when I didn't need space..even when I asked for it.

Thank you Partridge India, for helping me make a start.

A soulmate…in You..

I've heard that soulmates find
each other from wherever,
And once they meet, they never
let each other go again;
The bond is not conventional, but
that of a soul to a soul,
That rejoices in the ecstasy, and
feels the hurt and pain.
Someone who waits patiently before
He speaks his feelings,
Because once said..a soul remembers
a promise so true ;
That's the promise I see,
when I look into your eyes,
I wonder..Is it my soulmate
that I've found…in You?

 মঙ্গ   মঙ্গ   মঙ্গ

You're more honest, truer and more
grounded than I can ever be,
You are like my anchor, holding on
to me..before I lose my way;
Your embrace is my home..where I
can be safe from all harm,
And I could wake to the truth of
your eyes..every single day.
I love you for the way you see
nothing but good in everyone;
I love it..that You are simple at
heart, with no malice at all,
I love you for the way you see beauty
in me and not my scars,
I love it..that I can trust You to
catch me if I break or fall.

സ്റ്റോ   സ്റ്റോ   സ്റ്റോ

Suhasini Ramakrishnan

Bliss…is feeling your palms caress
mine..till I lose myself,
Love..is to feel the touch of your
warm palms on my face.
Ecstasy..is to see you smile at me..
when I open my eyes,
My sanctuary is the safety of your
wide and strong embrace.
Your love is not colored with any
personal need or judgement,
Your caress is passionate and soft..
still burns every part of me.
Your touch isn't rough to hurt, it
is full of warmth and care,
You hold me close, but not to tie
me down..but to set me free.

– Suhasini..
2nd Nov 2015

Aimless..

Always a gnawing need to know and understand
what is happening around me,
Always a restlessness that there is not
enough time to do what I want to do;
Always a feeling that someone or something
was left unattended by me today,
Always a feeling of being in the same rut,
to break away to find something new.
Always a bit of weird emptiness, a bit of
vacuum that sucks a bit of joy away,
Always a faraway thought in my eyes, for
which a reason I cannot seem to find;
A melody that is stuck in my head, but
does not make my soul want to sing,
Always the need to wait and look for what
slipped away, the urge to look behind.

Ò Ò Ò

Yet, there are those words "Look ahead, aim
for what you want to achieve today",
The "drive" that is meant to set us apart
from the ones who do not "achieve";
To weed away what pulls us away from
the "Goal", like dreams and wishes,
To segregate the important and unimportant,
emotions fall through the sieve.
The burning "Aim" that sometimes I don't
even recognize as what I want or need,
The "Destination" that I am not sure is
what I set for myself as my "Own goal";
The "Pinnacle" that I surmounted..but does
not make me feel like I am a victor,
I may have achieved what I was prescribed
to achieve ..but I still don't feel whole.

Ò Ò Ò

That is when I began to wonder if an "Aim"
is nothing but a material gain & loss,
If such kind of "Aims" fulfill my soul or
make sense to my other life at all ;
If these "Aims" really make me more complete,
or just add to the notches of wins,
Are these "Aims" defining my person, giving
meaning to every victory & every fall.
Sometimes when I walk "Aimlessly", I find
old paths that I used to happily tread,
Sometimes when I gaze "Aimlessly", I see
a face I had forgotten form in the cloud;
Sometimes when I think "Aimlessly", I
remember a promise that I broke long ago,
Sometimes when I hum "Aimlessly", I find
words of a song that I used to sing aloud.

Ò Ò Ò

Suhasini Ramakrishnan

Being Aimless lets me see how serenely lovely
the mountains I've being climbing are,
How they don't need to "Go" somewhere,
for they are at peace with where they are;
Being Aimless lets me feel the breeze, dance
with the waves, and sing with my soul,
See my dreams shimmering softly and calling
to me through the starlight from afar.
Being Aimless makes me find the child
and woman living somewhere inside,
Being Aimless makes me realize that not being
"driven" is not all that sinfully wrong;
It makes the universe reach out, whisper
to me, take me by my hand and lead,
Aimlessness lets my soul take me to a place
where my dreams matter and I truly belong.

– Suhasini
(19th Jan. 2015)

Always You..

Every waking morning, I will always
think of what you see in me,
Do I still warm your heart the way I
used to in the years gone by?
Do you still think about me when you
are driving home each day?
Do I still smile back at you when
you gaze at the azure sky?
Do the songs that we shared still make
you smile when you are alone?
Does the drizzle that kiss you, still
feel like me playing with you?
Do you remember the way you would
look at me & make me blush?
..Do you still feel that You belong
to me & I was made for You?

೧೩೫ ೧೩೫ ೧೩೫

This is what you said to me in the
early first weeks of our meeting,
Where you admired that I was not a
"usual girl", but fresh & bold;
That we could talk and laugh as old
friends and yet yearn as lovers,
That this comfort & understanding
between us will never grow old.
For we have matured and changed over
the years we've been together,
I don't ask for you for all the little
things that way I once used to;
I will always feel your arms around
me when I need to feel secure,
..the one whom I will trust implicitly
will always be You.

ಅಲ್ಲಿ   ಅಲ್ಲಿ   ಅಲ್ಲಿ

You are with me..and I know that
to be the one truth of my life,
And I will belong to You forever
with all of my heart and soul;
I thought that we don't need words
to say "I Love You" anymore,
And don't need to "touch" to know
that You make me whole.
Of late it hurts me to see you moving
farther away from me..bit by bit,
I've heard you say, "You're OK..
You don't need me anymore";
I do.. I will always and never stopped
needing you in my life,
To every turbulent emotion of mine..
You are my sanctuary..my shore.

લ૭ઝ૦   લ૭ઝ૦   લ૭ઝ૦

You are the one I draw my strength
from, my unshakeable rock,
You are my raincloud, caressing away
every one of my tears & pain;
..The touch of your roughness
against my cheek is bliss,
It makes me want not give up on Us..
to get up and try once again.
You alone can hear the screams that
hide behind my fake smile,
You are my hope, my anchor, my
faith, my truth, my rainbow;
You alone can make me smile, when
I want to break down & cry,
Always and forever You and only
You... I hope you know.

ℭℜℬℭ   ℭℜℬℭ   ℭℜℬℭ

You're the only one whose arms I
want around me at all times,
It is Your assurance is what keeps me
from breaking from within;
You're the surety..the trust, if I
choose to run away from it all,
You're the embrace that I want steadying
me.. whether I lose or win.
You are the sunshine..that warms me
when the world is cold to me,
..Your shoulder is my solace, when
my tears start to fall;
Your brown eyes..which I look into..
and find myself safe & secure,
Without You ..it isn't worth
believing in Love at all.

– Suhasini
(9th April 2015)

Someday..

You see me every single day, when
I walk past your door and smile,
I know that you wait for me, because
you are always surely there;
You look up, as if you were busy..
but happened to glance my way,
Then you smile knowingly..and I know
you're not going anywhere.
It is always the same..every single
day, like some daily ritual,
But not as if we do it for the sake of
it, but there is so much care;
One knowing glance, one wistful
smile, one fleeting moment,
So many stories in that moment...
like there is so much to share.

೫೪൭ ೫೪൭ ೫೪൭

You stay in my thoughts long after
I stop seeing your face,
You smile haunts me through all
that I do in the entire day;
The lines at the end of your eyes
belie your long harsh life,
Your hardened look tells me, that
you've pushed people away.
You intrigue me; make me wonder
and make me think too much,
A bit of an enigma..a mystery and
a touch of past unknown;
You seem to me like a horizon
untouched, a vast endless plain,
A glacial lake, a lone ranger, a
hermit..who is always alone.

ℭℬ ℭℬ ℭℬ

And then amidst all that I have to
remember, organize and do,
Somewhere, your thoughts as if
sublimate into the noon and eve;
You appear in my thoughts again,
I search for your presence,
Look at the place you sit, as if see if
it matters to you that I leave.
You are there, still silent, watchful,
waiting, patient and unmoving,
And I feel a stab of guilt, that I don't
give you more of my day;
Yet, your stature is just as calm, aloof
yet caring and composed,
As if to tell me that you are here, long
after all is over..here to stay.

୯୨୫୭   ୯୨୫୭   ୯୨୫୭

I think sometimes..of how would it
be if we spoke to one another,
Would we find something common
between us ? A tale for two?
Will those wistful smiles turn to
actual laughter for both of us?
Will the enigma I see..melt into a
story when I finally meet you?
And then I feel this stab of apprehension,
that I should not tease,
I should not disturb a beautiful
relationship for the want of more;
If the wave really aches to be one with
land, it will eventually happen,
Then the wave will traverse the ocean
and finally kiss her shore.

ಞಞ   ಞಞ   ಞಞ

Suhasini Ramakrishnan

When I finish thinking and look
at you sitting exactly there,
Your eyes soften..as if you know
what went on in my mind ;
And for the first time in so long,
you scribble on a letter-pad,
You look at me, sign and fold it, and
carefully leave it behind.
Then as you look at me and gesture
to the letter and stand up,
My heart as if missed a beat that day..
as if a dream came true;
I know you saw my face and smiled
at my reaction to this,
But I really wanted to know a little
more about the enigma in You.

સ્ર સ્ર સ્ર

The letter said everything I had hoped
it would say in words & feelings,
You were and are every bit the Man I
had dreamt that you would be;
I was your enigma, I was your
unfulfilled wish and your dream
You are someone with whom I could
feel safe, lose myself & yet be Me.
Not that we are teenagers today, love is
"deep" not "ebullient" anymore,
Our smiles are tinged with experience
& white hair with passing age;
When I look into the mirror, its as if
I look at a lost part of my heart,
As if Its your story in every book,
every chapter and in every page.

ॐ੬੭   ॐ੬੭   ॐ੬੭

I picked up the letter, looked around
to see if you were watching,
I couldn't see you anywhere but I
knew that your eyes were on me;
Something told me that you were
waiting to watch my reaction,
You were somewhere, out of my eyesight
but from where you could see.
All the letter said..was a word..it made
my eyes fill up with warmth,
As if you could read my apprehension
and wouldn't push me away;
I smiled and let my tears of gratitude
fall, so that you could see,
It wasn't just one word..but a promise.
All it said was.. "Someday"..

– Suhasini
(8th April 2015)

With Age...

Age provides a perspective that redefines
a lot what I think of the past,
Not everything that I lost in life was earth
shattering or really a loss to me;
Not all that I call "mine" today, is really
all that important or precious,
Nor is all that I want..going to complete
me, fulfil me or set me free.
But with Age..I've learnt to accept the
learnings from my past and present,
I've tried to understand what kind of
person I "truly am", not "claim to be";
I've sort of..given up on explaining or
justifying my views or self to others,
I've stopped trying to discover the world..
and am trying to discover "Me".

৪৯৫ ৪৯৫ ৪৯৫

Suhasini Ramakrishnan

I've discovered that coffee is a constant
companion that warms my heart,
A lot more than the company of people
who listen to reply..not understand;
I've discovered that I don't need "ladders"
to further myself in this world,
All the future I need is with me, is
already in the palm of my own hand.
I've learned that sometimes..I need to
wait out the fear and uncertainty,
"Doing something" does not always
guarantee that a problem can be solved;
With Age..I've learnt that "Activity" is
necessary sometimes but not always,
It is not the world that has changed ..but
my person that has evolved.

൩൦   ൩൦   ൩൦

I've discovered that Joy does not need a
situation, a premise or a fixed time,
That patience is a virtue only when there
is understanding, respect and love;
That happiness is choice, a state of mind,
not merely an external emotion,
Sometimes all the strength I need..
comes from looking at the sky above.
That cuddling up with a good book
can be the best kind of sabbatical,
That walking and singing in the rain
is a fabulous therapy for my soul;
With Age..I've learnt that people will
come and they will fade away,
If I rely on them to define my path and
joy, I will never feel or be whole.

രുജ്ഞ   രുജ്ഞ   രുജ്ഞ

Suhasini Ramakrishnan

I've learnt that it is my "wants" that
are many, my "needs" are few,
And it is these many "wants" that make
me restless and hold me tied;
It's this constant fighting fate that
makes life bitter, difficult and sad,
Maybe life would be simpler if I don't
fight, but go along for the ride.
I've seen that Ambition is good as
long as it doesn't influence life,
Drive and purpose are great till I know
when and where to draw a line;
With Age..I've learnt to take a seat back
sometimes in my life to breathe,
That I don't need to be there at the centre
of all or to burn out or to shine.

CR&D CR&D CR&D

Age is not always a bad thing, a warning
number or a lot of white hair,
For me..it has brought with it many
questions that I'd like to know;
It has brought maturity to leave some
stones unturned, some roads alone,
And has given me clarity on where I
want to be and where I want to go.
With Age..I've learnt to be my own
person, than to please everyone,
With Age..I've learnt that letting go is
as important as holding on to;
But..Most of all with Age..I've learnt
that nothing is unconditional,
And learnt that "cherishing the old" is as
important as "embracing the new".

ෙෂ   ෙෂ   ෙෂ

Suhasini Ramakrishnan

I've learnt that I should speak my mind
politely without compromising;
I've learnt that I should always say
"No", when my heart says "No";
I've learnt not to call "friends", who
don't touch my heart as people,
I've learnt that life is too short to
venture where I do not want to go.
I have begun to like my life quieter,
less busy and more purposeless,
I've begun to see merit in the voice of
silence that talks off and on to me;
With Age..I've begun to hear "that little
voice in my head" more often now,
Finally..I've warmed to the comfort of
being "ok"..just by being with me.

– Suhasini
(28th May 2015)

A getaway…with You..

Lush green cliffs, covered with mist & clouds,
Where the tops of mountains kiss the smiling sky;
Where the sun rises through the haze of mist,
Where in the haze of clouds…dewdrops rise and fly.
Where the dawn is ushered in by the sleepy breeze,
And the hills reply to the waking golden sunshine;
A place where nature answers the call of God,
A place where I'm only yours, & you are only mine.

ॐ ॐ ॐ

Suhasini Ramakrishnan

Faraway when the birds
play with the hilltops,
We sit cozy in each other's
loving & warm embrace;
Where I reach out and fill
all of you into my arms,
Where I can reach up..and see
your little angelic face.
Where I call out your name and
it echoes all around,
Where all I can hear is
your name again & again;
Where You and me are
together & with each other,
Amidst hazy mist, wisps of
clouds & droplets of rain.

CR80   CR80   CR80

Golden sunsets, set against
the backdrop of hills,
Our footprints..imprinted as
one on the golden sand;
Dancing on the patterns that the
waves draw on the shore,
Walking on the beach, at peace..
holding your little hand.
To be woken up by the spray of
the sea on our being,
To be able to watch the sky kiss
& merge with the sea;
To open my eyes & see you sleeping
soundly by my side
To awaken, to the cocoon of your
little arms around me.

☙❧   ☙❧   ☙❧

Suhasini Ramakrishnan

The edges of the earth bordering
on the steps of the sky,
Lazy twilights in the middle
of a long lost lagoon;
You..smiling at me,
with your little innocent face,
Long evenings..lost in the mellow
light of the moon.
Soft whispers..in which I read
bedtime stories to you,
Loud heartbeats..a mother and child
merging & becoming One;
Dreams of this bond lasting
across lifetimes & births,
Shadows of a glorious life..in the
light of the mellow sun.

ೞ಩ ೞ಩ ೞ಩

Someday, your little hand will
grow to hold my frail palm,
And guide me through roads that
one I led you through;
I hope you will see the pride in
my eyes, my little one,
And I hope you know..that I gave
my everything to You.
I hope for everlasting love and
understanding for one another,
Everlasting trust that you will hold
my hand honest & true;
A bond that grows..from a mother,
to a guide and end as a friend,
I pray, that in every life, my blessings
rest in and with YOU.

– Suhasini
17th December 2010

A long wait..

My eyes still look at the
path that you once tread,
My tears still wait, to moisten
your shoulders again;
My wasted wait to whisper "I
love you" in your ears,
My being yearns for you to hold
me..and erase this pain.
Skies have gone from a
golden azure to ashen grey,
Seasons from glorious spring to
winter..cold and blue;
My smile has frozen..for it does
not touch my lips anymore,
My life has as if withered & stilled..
in this wait for You.

❧ ❧ ❧ ❧ ❧

I love only you..and someday..
hoped to have all your love,
Look at a life with all of you..
not just a part of You;
Look into your eyes..and not see
unfinished deeds in them,
Hold your hands..and know that
this clasp is forever true.
To create a life with you..and
live a lifetime as yours,
As I hope you will live a lifetime
with only me in your heart;
All this wait, distance, adjustment
& separation today,
So that we can be together tomorrow
& never have to part.

৶৶৶৶৶

Suhasini Ramakrishnan

I hope you see the ache
that holds me back a little,
The invisible cord that pulls me
little away from you;
I hope you hear the unsaid
words coming my soul,
The hope for you to be only mine,
the way I belong to you.
I hope someday you are proud to
accept & cherish my love,
Believe that I've done for you all
that I could possibly do,
I hope you feel the uncertainty
in my heart and erase it,
I hope someday you believe &
trust the love I have for You.

ॐ ॐ ॐ ॐ ॐ

Today, it looks to me that I'm
fighting a losing battle,
Only I wish to be together
forever, as One..someday;
I keep praying the sun rises on
one such a glorious dawn,
You seem to have walked away
long ago, and I still stay.
It looks to me that I'm giving it
all, the love and care,
I know you aren't waiting and
that you don't share pain;
This is killing me.. I'm done with
this thankless long wait,
I deserve a chance to let go..and
find myself once again.

৯৯৯৯৯

I will put myself together again,
stronger and wiser,
This time, I will know, how not
to hurt myself again;
I will know truly if a broken heart
mends, but remembers,
I will know if this wait, lesson
and hurt is not in vain.
I will learn whether a long wait
means a deeper scar,
Or if it is just a wait.. with emptiness
and even more pain;
Somehow.. I believe that this wait
will teach me even more,
And I will never be a victim to a
wasted long wait..ever again.

– Suhasini
12th November 2010

A world without numbers..

Sometimes I wonder…what would a
world without numbers be like,
Would we still feel the need to "grade",
"weigh against" and "rate"?
Will we still "compare" our all the
types of love in our limited life?
Would we still "count" the gifts that
our life served into our plate?

Will "Age" be just a number that
denotes how old we have become?
Or will it denote the mature richness
with which we lived our life?
Will our wrinkles be "counted" as
lines if maturity and experience?
Or will they just be counted as a
lifetime of wasted tears and strife?

③ 🕒 ❽

Suhasini Ramakrishnan

Will an "Incentive" or "Increment" tell
us how successful we truly are?
Will "Salary" be a measure of the
height of true success and fame?
Will our knowledge be graded by number
of examinations we give & pass?
Will a commercial tag of "Band", "Rating"
& "CTC" replace our name?

③ 🕐 ❽

Tell me..Will minutes and seconds be
the measure of our togetherness?
Will a clock dictate the number of
hours that I can be with You?
Will an anniversary be just a "duration"
spent walking with each other?
Or will it be reminiscing moments where
we professed our feelings true?

③ 🕐 ❽

Will we "log-in" the count of times we
thought of & missed each other?
Will we fight over the number of promises
kept and number of failed tries?
Without numbers..we won't "number"
the days spent in hapless wait,
A night will elapse..looking from within
your embrace at the starlit skies.

③ 🕐 ❽

Would "Years" be a "measure" of time
that unknowingly passed by us?
Or will it be a treasure of little moments
that I spent holding Your hand;
A lifetime will mean when our smile
will explain all that we need to say,
Time will just be a temporary wave that
drew patterns on the shifting sand.

③ 🕐 ❽

Someday..when we can rise above the
world of numbers controlling us,
Maybe we will truly see the moments
of joy and tears that we didn't see,
Maybe hours in the day won't pull us back
from spending time with each other,
Maybe the clock won't dictate count of
moments spent between You and Me.

③ 🕐 ❽

Numbers won't put perspective to how
time stretched when You weren't there,
Because numbers will not help me tell
you that my love for You is still true;
There are no numbers that can fathom
the depth of our togetherness,
There are no numbers to count the ways
in which I love and still miss You.

– Suhasini
(8th November 2012)

Abjection..

I have neither words,
nor any hopes in me now,
No questions, no answers,
no anger, no tears;
No dreams, no sunsets,
no paths of glory,
No wait, no explanations,
no strength, no fears.
No precious thoughts
of motivation for the future,
No rainbow tinted
horizons that I can see;
I don't know if there is
merit in goodness at all,
Nor do I know if there
is any persistence left in me.

%%%%

Suhasini Ramakrishnan

I don't know if there will
be a shore for my storm,
Or if a storm is all that
I am destined in to sail;
I do not know if my sky
will ever clear to the sun,
Or against rocks, the strength
of my raft will fail.
Why is it that when I am
at the helm for others,
The ship sails strong,
sure and emerges free;
Why is it that when I try
to sail one of my dreams,
The horizon and shore I seek..
I cannot remotely see.

%%%%

When there is no hope,
nor any expectation within,
There is mindless peace and
numbing silence all around;
When I ask of when peace and
joy will be from within,
All I hear is deathly silence, not
a murmur..not a sound.
There are insinuations that it is
all the ghost of my faults,
Why?? Have I never done
a single good deed at all?
If making people happy is
something You smile upon,
Haven't I not played my part ..
however meagre or small?

%%%

I ask you today, is it a sin to
ask for a little happiness,
A transgression to hope
to complete ones heart;
Is it a folly to see my dreams
in each other's eyes,
To hurt and miss each one
other, when far apart.
Abjection is not just for today,
but for many such days,
When I have not known what to
change, to do or to say;
Abjection is this feeling of restlessness,
of inaction and loss,
what more I could have done to
not have ended up this way

– Suhasini
(3rd Dec. 09)

Till death do us apart..

I can see it slip out of my palms,
I can see my tears getting lost in the brine;
I can see that there won't be spring anymore,
I can see that you can never be mine.
I can see that all I get is hurt, I can
see that love is not meant to be;
I can see that it selflessness is a waste, I can
see that you will never belong to me.
I can see that faith does not bear fruit;
that patience is not always a virtue;
I can see the horizon, but it is barren,
Because in the sunset.. I cannot see you.
Days of waiting turned into months,
and months into years they grew;
But for all the honest faith and the true
wait, My hand is not clasped by you.

&&&

I wanted to give you every joy in the world,
Tried so hard to never ask you for much;
I yearned for a few moments of your time,
for the warmth of the occasional touch.
But the most expensive gift of all is Time, once
given, moments can't ever be returned;
Thank you for every unforgettable memory,
every lesson of selfless love that I learned.
It hurts.. I will not lie that it does not, But for
you.. I will do all that makes you smile;
You've touched my heart the way no one has,
The moving away might take a while.
But I do not want to be the reason for your
guilt, the reason for your heartache;
Let your heart take all my joy, happiness
and cheer, I will pay for my mistake.

&&&

Do you honestly think I could last away from
you, and my heart will ever beat again?
Do you think I will ever trust anyone once
more, or staying away will ease the pain?
You have taught me a precious lesson that
it is never good be selfless in love;
This hurt will remind every single day, the
lesson will sparkle in the night sky above.
I shall still believe in love as long as I
live, For I have loved honest & true;
For every tear I shed.. there will be an
answer somewhere..away from you.
Years will diminish the pain inside and
Time will heal this scar on my heart,
Never again will I say with each and
every breath.. "Till death do us apart."

– Suhasini
(8th May 08)

Introspection & Peace

Not a long saga...but a full one is how
I'd describe my life, if ever asked,
Lots of things seen, heard, felt, yet lots
left to feel, learn and understand;
Many wounds have now healed, for I
see them in a new light.. unbiased,
I know that life about the experience, that
there is no reward or reprimand.
There's moments of ecstasy, and moments
of abject despair..yet both pass,
What remains is the learning, the maturity
gained and the wisdom of age;
That my path is as I make it, filled with
contentment or disappointment,
That my life is as I create it.. unfettered
or the confined in a self made cage.

෴ ෴ ෴

So many incidents that I let rankle within..
are actually inconsequential,
That many things holding me back are
a waste..became clear in retrospect;
If only I saw that in the future..these
wouldn't really matter to me at all,
If only I looked within a little earlier, if
only didn't react..but did introspect.
So, I made a little castle in my already
crowded and confused head,
To see if I could sort out the wheat from
the chaff and wish the bad away;
I found so many moments that I was
delighted to be in, be a part of,
That the hurt vanished and it was as if..
contentment came home to stay.

❧ ❧ ❧

Suhasini Ramakrishnan

It's amazing how when the rose tinted
glasses come off, the world is better,
Expectations are reined in, hopes are
practical and demands are set right;
I expect less, so I get more; ask for less,
so I seem to have so much with me,
For once I set my mind at ease with my
own self, the world does seem bright.
The horizon does not look far away or out
of reach, like it used to in the past,
It looked like another home, waiting for
me, at the other side of the shore;
There are no tears, no unfinished business,
no yearning, no empty feelings,
There is completeness, fulfillment, calm
and eternal peace forevermore.

– Suhasini
(12ᵗʰ June 2013)

DUSK....

A silent cloak of days gone by,
A wreath of old memories;
A shriveled shroud of past moments,
laid out on dry autumn leaves.
This is how my days go by, and
how I wait for night to fall;
This is how the DUSK of my life looks;
Surrounded by no one at all.
I am enveloped by this deathly silence,
The ashen sky covers the earth;
Embers have sighed and died down,
Only ashes cover the hearth.
Wilted branches of dead trees,
Break off painfully and fall;
Mountains mourn in patient wait,
Thirsting for an echo to call.
Starless, painfully gaping night skies,
Yearn for the light of the moon;
Dry, desultory winds embrace, Every
cold, mourning sand dune.
This is how the DUSK looks without you,
eyes unmoving, cold and dead as stone.
A cadaver of emotions, feelings and
wants, In wait, solitary and alone

– Suhasini
1st June 2008

Despair..

When the earth in my heart was arid,
There was no hurt, no ache and no pain;
Yes, it was solitary, but not lonely, No
emotion, no blessings, no rain.
No oasis of false hopes and dreams, No
mirages that I reached out to hold;
No sun, no breeze, only frigid ice to touch,
I had made peace with the biting cold.
When a path presented itself to me, It
came with thorns; I knew it to be so;
No Eden, no home, no sanctuary, no rest,
Only desert as far as my vision would go.
My mind a tyrant, keeping me in check, My
heart..an enemy prodding me to trust;
A thick wall of forbidden feelings around me,
a heart and soul of stone had become a must.

ৡৣ৵ৣ৵ৣ৵ ৡৣ৵ৣ৵ৣ৵ ৡৣ৵ৣ৵ৣ৵

Eyes always tinted with salty tears, Yet a
resolve emboldened with hurt & pain;
Alone, yet in sole control of where I am, From
begging, asking for help did I abstain.
Dreams never bothered my disturbed sleep,
Comfort never threatened my rocky trail;
Laughter tried, but never touched my soul, Hope
would try to entice, but would always fail.
When I first heard you knock on my heart,
I did not believe the herald to be true;
Never imagined that my hand would be
held, that my destination could be You.
Never trusted that love would win over despair,
Never trusted that my heart would feel;
Never imagined that hope would tinge my
horizon, that my scars would start to heal.

৯৯৯৯   ৯৯৯৯   ৯৯৯৯

Suhasini Ramakrishnan

Trust sears more than not trusting the world,
Somehow..hope hurts more than despair;
My heart is used to being ignored and stabbed,
What makes it bleed is the warmth and care.
I had stopped asking questions to myself,
Stopped looking for answers to my fears;
Stopped treading down paths with dead ends,
Stopped waiting for anyone to wipe my tears.
Today, I doubt my own questions and doubts,
Question my capability to hold on & let go;
Can I surrender myself completely to you?
Can I feel with a full heart? I don't know.
Stopped looking back to see a familiar shadow,
Stopped looking for a horizon to walk into;
Stopped looking at myself in another's eyes,
All these.. I've begun to hope for..with You.

৩৯৯ ৩৯৯ ৩৯৯

Can I give you what you've waited for? Can
I look into your eyes & read your heart?
Can I love? Can I urge myself to love more?
Can I stay anymore.. without you.. apart?
Can I say that I am complete all by myself?
No.. I cannot.. I am alive only with you;
I was never living.. it was just existing,
What I was doing till now wasn't true.
Is it wise to open the doors to my heart like
this? Do I if it will it not hurt again?
Will I be able to rise above the doubt, the
past, the and the nagging fear of pain?
Today.. my wilted heart responds to love, My
scarred soul responds to your tender care;
My faith sings along with your song of belief,
Your love dispels my shroud of despair.

– Suhasini
(7th January 09)

Suhasini Ramakrishnan

Echoes..

A distant call, a name humming
deep within my heart,
A faraway, yet familiar voice that
keeps echoing in my ears;
A soft whisper..yet a voice loud
enough to make me believe,
An assurance of someone being
there..allaying my fears.
I know not if is this is your voice
that I hear inside me?
For I know that no other
voice can reach my heart;
It has to be your calm, soft yet
true and honest voice,
Inspiring me…convincing me
on to make a fresh start.

❀&❀   ❀&❀

Lost voices calling out from a
broken, shattered past,
Shards of painful memories piercing
my horizon, my sight;
I hear your voice resonating in
the depths of my soul,
A whisper, an echo.. telling me
that it will be alright.
For every thread of my past that
keeps pulling me back,
I will reach out and hold
your outstretched hand;
No more echoes of my past will
haunt me ever again,
With the strength of my faith
in you..will I stand.

❋&❋　❋&❋

Wait is a leveler and it
makes me truly understand,
It makes me see the place you
have in every day of mine;
It shows me how much of you are
alive in every moment,
How it is your smile that ushers
in my day, my sunshine.
So, I hold the lamp of faith
in my palm of my hand,
And, I hold the lamp of faith in
the seashell of my eyes;
It is only your love brightens
my faith and my life.
Like the full moon lights up the
darkness of the skies.

❋&❋   ❋&❋

It is but a cold, dead winter
without you in my life,
As if the days went back to being
grey and meaningless;
As if the nights were meant to wait
listlessly for another dawn,
Nothing to look forward to in life,
wasted and worthless.
But, ever since I've filled tears
of your love in my eyes,
There are colours so vivid,
beautiful, heartfelt and true;
The melody of your love
echoes in my heart & soul,
I keep the lamp of wait alive
in my heart.. for You.

❅&❅   ❅&❅

Suhasini Ramakrishnan

Your truth and confidence
radiates from your being,
Your honesty and truth shine
forth in all that you do;
Your commitment and
humanness is for all to see,
I find none as down to earth
and dependable as You.
These are not mere words, don't
regard them trivially,
These are testaments to your
integrity and resolve today;
These resounding echoes of your
strength of character,
Will continue to sound, long
after you've gone away.

❄&❄   ❄&❄

For echoes are not mere
intonations of lost words,
They are a testimony to what
people will say for you;
They are proofs etched
on the monoliths of age,
Not a word on falsehood,
every syllable being true.
Echoes of unadulterated love
for you in so many eyes,
Only echoes of reaffirmation
everywhere I can find;
Look up..it's your name
and footprint everywhere,
Echoes resounding that You..
are and will be one of kind.

– Suhasini
(13th January 2010)

Suhasini Ramakrishnan

Emptiness...

To be able to see and
know that it cannot belong,
To hurt.. but know that
the wound will never heal;
To hold words back..
for the want of understanding,
To break within.. but to act
as if one does not feel.
A desert of dreams
thirsting to come true,
Parched eyes looking up
at the arid sky in vain;
Elsewhere where there
is a need for an anchor,
There is boundless abundance
of tears and rain.

Ц Ц Ц

To know that the road
will forever be empty,
That there will be no-one
to walk it with me;
To know that no-one
will be there to talk to,
Only miles and miles
of silent, unbroken sea.
To scream and know
that it will not be heard,
To shed tears.. only to
mingle with the brine;
To bleed and know
that it will not stop,
To yearn for someone
to hold & call mine..

Ц Ц Ц

To laugh and know that
it is not from the heart,
To be afraid to feel with
the heart once again;
To not have your own
smile reach your eyes,
Each day.. to try and
make peace with pain.
This is emptiness.. that
lasts forever and ever,
This is the vacuum that
dries up the soul;
The lacuna that engulfs
ones zest to live,
And then.. life
ceases to be whole.

Ц Ц Ц

Each time I look into
your eyes.. I realize,
This is the hand I had
yearned to touch;
When I see you smile..
I know from within;
For someone like you…
I ache so much.
It is your smile makes me
want to believe,
It is your assurance
caresses my fears away;
I truly don't know
if you even realize,
That it is your warmth
that ushers in my day.

Ц Ц Ц

Suhasini Ramakrishnan

Smile.. and may
your smile last forever,
May there never be
a crease on your brow;
May every bud bloom
when you cross its path,
May heaven with
choicest blessings endow.
For, your joy …
fills up my emptiness,
And for a few moments,
my faith I regain;
You unknowingly give
me a moment of life,
Before I dissolve into
this emptiness again.

– Suhasini
(24th Feb. 08)

Everything misses you..

The dawn does not have
life anymore or warmth
The day is listless,
crestfallen, morose and dry;
The breeze is listless,
no fragrance, no melody in it,
Cloudless, grey, bleary,
bleak, ashen is the sky.
The gardens are as if stilled and
lifeless in themselves,
The flowers don't smile or dance
to the breeze like before;
The clouds don't play with the
sun and draw shadows,
Waves silently reach out and barely
touch the sandy shore.

♫♫♫♫

Suhasini Ramakrishnan

The rain as if is tears from the
heavy heart of the sky,
The wind wails mournfully..
laments the sunset;
Notes of the flute, segue with
the waning moonlight,
No echo from the hills
does my waiting call beget.
The searing sun burns both the
heart and the earth alike,
There is deathly silence around
in the midst of a busy day;
My breath comes and goes..
as if with no reason at all.
As if life itself has ceased
to be..when you are away.

♫♫♫♫

It is not that anything
has changed so dramatically,
But.. your being there is what
makes my ashen sky blue;
Everything in my life
misses you so very much,
As if the life of the whole world..
is wrapped up in YOU.
I miss you.. and it sears
and hurts so very much,
My heart feels arid.. a desert..
parched for the want of rain;
I never knew that I could feel
this much of love in me,
Thank you..for making me believe
in love..once again.

– Suhasini
(12th October 2010)

Hope…

Hope floats even when the last
blade of support sinks,
Hope is eternal and lasts
long after despair dies;
Hope is that light at the end
of a long dark tunnel,
Hope is the promise,
lighting up my ashen skies.
Hope is faith, that these
tough times too shall pass,
and that the sun will filter
through the trees again;
Hope is that silver lining on
every cloud in our lives,
that assures us of lasting comfort
after this momentary pain.

Ψ Ψ Ψ

Hope for me is your clasp, that
holds my palm inside yours,
Hope for me is standing secure
in your arms in the rain;
Hope for me blossoms each time
you softly say "I Love You",
This Hope proves that our wait
true and is not in vain.
Hope for me is the melody I hear
from every sparkling star,
Hope for me is You...shining like the
Full moon in a dark night;
Hope is to be able to look into your
eyes & see myself smile,
Hope is knowing..that with You..
everything will be alright.

Ψ Ψ Ψ

Hope is knowing that distance
will not be a barrier,
Hope is trusting that time won't fade
my memories in your heart;
I will learn not become a shadow
and merge to be one with You,
Hope is trusting that never again,
do we have to be apart.
Hope is believing in each prayer that
I say with the rising dawn,
I hope for peace, calm and happiness
to come..with us to stay;
For togetherness and understanding
to filter into our lives,
And for everlasting understanding..
to illuminate each & every day.

– Suhasini
21st June 2010

Horizon

When the red twilight sun,
starts to sink,
When the tired evening sky
rests against the sea;
When the weary birds
move homewards,
And there is a azure tiredness
as far as eye can see..
The horizon too beckons
with open arms,
Calls out to the weary, spent,
tired and aching day;
The moon stands waiting
at the edge of the ocean;
Waiting for the last sun-ray
to silently slip away.

০২৪০   ০২৪০   ০২৪০

Suhasini Ramakrishnan

The horizon watches
me as I gaze into it,
The horizon smiles at my
unflinching hope in love;
The horizon says that
true love truly never meets,
Like the depth of the sea
aches for the sky above.
I smile at the horizon &
look heavenward,
To see vermillion where
it once was blue;
My tears have blended
into the ocean,
And my heart has
bled in wait for you..

– Suhasini
(29th June 2007)

I wish You could..

I wish You could understand the
feelings behind what's left unsaid,
Sometimes, I wish You knew that
words cannot express it all;
Sometimes.."I trust You" can mean
just that You will hold my secret,
Sometimes it means I believe that You'll
catch my tears before they fall.
Sometimes, being broken and rising
from the ashes can mean perfect,
because You'd know how deep hurt can
go and how long it takes to heal;
because You'd know that my silence has
a louder voice than what is spoken..
Sometimes, I wish You'd know that it
is true & is beyond the way I feel.

¥ ¥ ¥

I run away, because it is better to be rough
and alive, than sensitive and hurt,
But, I am awe of people who are not
afraid to hurt and feel once again;
I don't reach out anymore, because it
either stays empty, or scalds my palm,
I don't want pick up pieces of me all my
life, or to make peace with the pain.
I'm tired of covering parched feelings
with a reluctant mirage of false hope,
I'm tired of watching dreams fade away
when they still mean much to me;
I don't look back at where I came from,
because I know the road will be empty,
I'd rather be alone than lonely, rather not
be bound in promise, I'd rather be free.

¥ ¥ ¥

There are too many scars, too many cracks
between which my emotions fell,
There are too many promises meant to
be kept, that painfully broke away;
There were too many questions, for which
I've never found answers till date,
Too many spring-times faded, which
I thought were meant to stay.
Still, all of me inside isn't dead, there
are remnants of what I used to feel,
I still smile and cry, I'm still touched by
surprises, I still respond to care;
I still yearn, I still sing, I still try to find
colours in imaginary rainbows,
Somewhere inside a moribund shell, I
hope that few emotions are still there..

– Suhasini
(31st Oct. 2012)

Loneliness...

Miles and miles of
unbroken burnt sand,
Tears cried and spent, mingling
with the unbroken sea;
Now I have no feelings
or emotions left,
No traces of hope, trust,
faith or wait left in me.
No wanting to see
another day's sun rise,
Nothing new to see in the
stars or the moonlight;
No sadness for the breaking
of a treasured dream,
After all, dreams end with
the death of the night.

෨෨෨

My sun rises to burn
all traces of tears and dew,
So that my heart awakens
so as not to feel;
I do not believe that scars
fade away with time,
I do not believe that
these cracks will heal.
Why wait to see if
I can hear footfalls,
I do not want to believe
that it will ever rain;
Why sow a seed, nourish,
caress and let it grow,
Only to watch it wilt,
shrivel and die in pain.

৵৵৵৵

Suhasini Ramakrishnan

How is it, that one can
live a lie every single day,
And yet laugh as if every
living moment is true;
How can it be that I look
forward to nothing?
Yet appear as if I welcome
every sunrise new.
When this heavy lie is
lived and life is done,
When I'm done walking this road
and singing this song,
I will disappear unnoticed
into nothingness,
Into the peace of oblivion..
in which I truly belong..

– Suhasini
(23rd September 09)

Love

Is Love a measure of how much
I soar in the skies with I'm with You?
Or is Love a measure of how soulfully
deep for You, do my feelings run?
Is Love that nameless smile, that vague
warmth or that constant song in me?
Is Love knowing in the deepest part of
my heart that "Yes.. He is the One!!"

❧ ❧ ❧

Or is Love pining for You..wanting to
know what it feels like to be wanted,
Is Love living the hurt of something I
lost, and re-living it every single day;
Or is Love that secret wish, that I dream
of each night & wake to each dawn?
Or is Love a lifetime of silently waiting
to be swept off my feet someday?

❧ ❧ ❧

Suhasini Ramakrishnan

Can I truly define Love? Am I that
mature? Can I claim to be that wise?
Can Love be described, confined, explained
& limited? Is that what is true?
I think now..that Love is knowing that
You're always &
forever within me,
Love is not wanting
You to be mine..
Love is Wordlessly
Belonging to You.

– Suhasini
(19th Dec. 2012)

Prayers..

I pray that your hand
holds mine forever,
I pray that there always
care in your touch;
I pray that we walk together
till the end of time,
I pray that our love never
fades & stays just as much.
I pray that I never cease
to feel your heart,
I pray that I can fulfill your
need before you say;
I pray that only You stay
in my heart & soul,
I pray to wake to your
eyes every single day.

❄❄❄❄

Suhasini Ramakrishnan

I pray that I can
always make you laugh,
I pray that we grow
together into a lovely pair;
I pray that tough times yield to
our love and tenacity,
I pray that we never lose out on
the warmth and care.
I pray that we remain
a little childlike all life,
I pray that we always see the
silver lining on the cloud;
I pray that the streak of craziness
in us always stays,
I pray that laughter abounds in
our life..bold and loud.

❄❄❄❄

I pray that we see the
best always in each other,
I pray that time make us
appreciate each other more;
I pray that we realize how blessed
we are to be with each other;
I pray that our togetherness lasts
the sea of life, to the shore.
I pray that our eyes always
look onto each other,
I pray that distance never set our
hearts and soul apart;
I pray that we always run fondly
in each other's feelings,
I pray that our love beats forever
in each other's heart.

❁ ❁ ❁ ❁

Suhasini Ramakrishnan

I pray that our prayers for each
other are always blessed,
I pray that we always stay in the
shade of blessings divine;
I pray that we bring out the best
in each other forever,
I pray that our trust in each
other does always shine.
I pray that we always face life's
ups and downs together,
I pray that the faith we have in
each other stays true;
I pray that the love in our
clasps remains precious,
I pray that our love never pales..
remains forever new.

❅❅❅❅

I pray that we become
the strength for one another,
I pray that we, each other
faith in us renew;
I pray that the nights
of sadness don't last long,
I pray that our trust in each other
remains forever true.
I pray..that no trouble
ever touches you;
I pray that you emerge
victorious through it all;
I pray that you defeat
every adversity in life,
I pray that you stand
leonine, victorious & tall.

❄❄❄❄

Suhasini Ramakrishnan

I pray that this togetherness
lasts the test of time,
I pray that we leave
the world with each other;
I pray for togetherness
in both life and death;
I pray for pristine,
doubtless trust in one another.
I pray everyday.. that we
find our faces as a mirror,
I pray it reflects our love,
that is mature and true;
I pray that I make your life
an endless heaven,
I pray that in my life..
I forever and ever have YOU.

– Suhasini
(31st Dec. 09)

Precious

The Diamond that the earth
hides in her womb,
The Black Pearl the sea
secrets in her watery deep;
The Intoxicating Musk,
that a deer would die for,
Ancient Pristine Lore..
that time does sacred keep.
Blue Sapphire that a magician
treasures with life,
The Blood Ruby, so dear
to the serpent's heart;
The Untold treasures at
the edge of the oceans,
Sailors go in hope to acquire,
seven seas apart.
A Mystic spell that brings
forth a hidden gate,
To an Enchanted Castle,
a lost city of dreams;
The Fountain of Youth
that every man searches,

However distant its proof
of existence seems.
Mountains of jade, crafted
in faultless precision,
Novas of Stadust.. a Stellar
event to bless the skies;
Crystals of delicate snowflakes
and its designs,
Prismatic rainbows, etching
vibrant colors in my eyes.
The Healing Touch of an Oracle,
pristine & pure,
Untold of riches, hidden in
long lost caves of magic,
Nectar of the Milky way,
creasing the sky above;
All these precious things
of this world & the next,
Don't compare to the strength
of true precious love.

– Suhasini
25th January 2010

Relationships..

A string was tied to a few people with birth;
These relations are beyond precious,
You are the ones who will walk with me..
till the feet can move no more;
You are the ones who will share joys and
sorrows truthfully, and trust completely,
You are the rocks on which I anchor,
You are the rainbows beyond the shore.
You are the ones close enough to share,
And truly understand the pain of failure,
You bear the brunt of all disappointments,
You see the ugly side..and yet You care;
You watch as success is shared last with You..
yet You wish well and smile with me.
No matter how far away we may be,
there's always the surety..that You're there.

৺ ৶ ৺ ৶ ৺ ৶

Suhasini Ramakrishnan

All other relations are fragile.. are momentary,
are for some meaning or the other,
All other relationships are for a reason,
for a month, a year, a decade or two;
Your love is unconditional,
Your trust pristine,
Your support timelessly unstinting,
There is no relationship, no trust, no belief,
no prayer..more beautiful than You.
You lasted with me when hope, positivity,
time and tide & me were running against,
You touched me with love, when all I felt
only hatred in all that was around me;
We never said "I want space..I want to
be by myself" to each other ever,
An epitome of standing true by the one
You love, as true as one can truly be.

❧ ❧   ❧ ❧   ❧ ❧

It's true that relationships should be open,
spacious and not claustrophobic,
For that is truly when one finds where
one would want to stay and belong;
Where there is no concept of "You must do",
"You should do", but "I want to do",
Where there is celebration of what one
innately is, not nit picking for the wrong.
For I bind myself when the choice is mine, not
forced on or made for me by anyone else,
That is when I feel that my faults are accepted,
and I will improve on them, to not hurt You;
When You help me build a relationship with
myself, help me not hate myself so much,
That is when I realize that this relationship
is meant to be, and this bond is true.

❧ ❧   ❧ ❧   ❧ ❧

Suhasini Ramakrishnan

I love You for each time You forgive my
mistakes and help be become a better person,
I love You for the endless patience,
The understanding, the selfless love and the space;
I love You for sharing with me, moments of
insanity, days of ecstasy, nights of despair,
I love You for the maturity, tears of joy,
The peace in Your eyes and smile on Your face.
I love You for the way You make me feel that
You know You will be in my prayers,
I love You for the way You wordlessly
Define what a selfless relationship should be;
I love You for knowing me and still finding
something in me to appreciate and love,
I love You Mother..for the way
Your learning, love and blessing shines inside me.

– Suhasini
22nd July 2013

Silence..

It is not as if there is nothing being said
anymore between the two of us,
It is just that words don't form a part
of our conversations anymore;
You as if read my eyes, and as if know
the depth of my care and respect,
I can feel both the distance and the
closeness…the horizon & the shore.
The soft wisps of breeze are the soft
memories that caress my heart,
The rustle of the leaves, is Your whisper..
telling me.."Yes..I know";
The waves that touch me..remind me
that You will always be there,
Memories of You will moisten my
eyes..no matter how far I go.

ও ও ও

Suhasini Ramakrishnan

You pervade in each & every moment
of my life, be it awake or asleep,
So many things I do are reminiscent
something that you casually said;
I guess that is what care is all about..
remembering every little thing,
A smile for no reason..a twinkle in my
eyes..a lasting song in my head.
When You see me.. You know what I'm
smiling about & smile with me,
At that moment I feel as if this all the
understanding I will ever need;
This is what living is about..to understand
& be understood..as we are,
No aims to achieve, no destinations to
reach, no immaculate life to lead.

ৡ ৡ ৡ

So today.. I reach out to this warm
silence around me once again,
And I hear the soft lilting melody
of Your presence in my day;
An assurance that Your touch will make
it lovelier and more fragrant,
A promise..that You will color my life..
not just mar it & walk away.
When I open my eyes..I find You
looking back at me with warmth,
As if You know exactly what I wished
for..and pray that it comes true;
I know that we both treasure this
silence for its comfort & quiet,
You treasure it for moments with me &
I treasure it for moments with You.

ও ও ও

Suhasini Ramakrishnan

I love it when You smile when You
see...I remember what You like,
You will know that I will keep every
promise I ever made to You;
You will never need to tell me twice,
what makes You smile or sad,
You will always be in my thoughts,
in all that I think, say and do.
No more words do I need to tell you
what I feel & what's in my heart,
I know that You can hear it while it
is still pristine, unsaid & true;
Some things are so beautiful..they don't
need the support of words at all,
This silence between us is enough...
for my feelings to reach out to You.

– Suhasini
(6th Dec. 2012)

Wait…

It feels like a lonely walk
that lasts a whole lifetime,
It's a long walk along
life's wave kissed shore;
I see you in my heart, but don't
see you walk with me,
And this wait does not inspire
hope in me anymore.
The sun rises, shines, illuminates
and sets in the west,
This wait to be with you seems
to have no end at all;
My tears have fallen and
mingled with the brine,
When will you send for me?
When for me will you call?

Щ Щ Щ Щ

Suhasini Ramakrishnan

Every soft waves that runs
past my feet, stabs me,
Every little spray stings
my heart with its touch;
Each time the swell of
the sea caresses the sand,
I yearn for, long for and
miss you so very much.
I walk this shoreline alone
in this hour of sunset,
So that you cannot see how
much my heart has bled;
You will never know the
pain & ache in my heart,
That it's tears of my blood
colouring the horizon red.

– Suhasini
(16th June 2010)

Wonderful....

Some are wonderful because
they have external beauty,
Some are wonderful with
the beauty of the mind;
Some are wonderful for the ability
to carry hurt in them,
Some are wonderful for the strength
to leave hurt behind.
Some are wonderful for
the way they string words,
Some are wonderful for the
character of their being,
Some are wonderful for the way
they speak with their eyes;
Some are wonderful for the way
the help others in seeing.

ೞೞ ೞೞ ೞೞ

Suhasini Ramakrishnan

Some are wonderful for their ability
to make people laugh,
Some are wonderful for the way
they conceal their tears;
Some are wonderful for the way
they never give up in life,
Some are wonderful for the way
they surmount their fears.
Some are wonderful for the way
they keep life simple,
Some are wonderful for the way
they seem to live carefree;
Some are wonderful for the way
the rise again after a fall,
Some are wonderful for the way,
the best in life they see.

ଓୋ ଓୋ   ଓୋ ଓୋ   ଓୋ ଓୋ

Some are wonderful for the way
they keep hope within alive,
Some are wonderful for the way
they keep faith burning true;
Some are wonderful for the way they
make words dance on their lips,
Some are wonderful for the way their
presence ushers in hope anew.
Some are wonderful for the way they
make us feel proud of being us,
Some are wonderful..because they
are touched by the spirit above;
Some are wonderful because they
choose to believe despite the hurt,
Some are wonderful because.. fill the
air with the abundance of love.

– Suhasini
(13th October 2010)

You are to blame…

You are to blame for
the joy in my life,
You are to blame for
the sunshine in each day;
You are to blame for
the dreams that I see,
You are to blame for
the blossoms on my way.
You are to blame for
the softness in my eyes,
You are to blame for
my renewed belief in love;
You are to blame for
reviving my lost hopes,
You are to blame for the silver
lining in my sky above.

Ц Ц Ц Ц

You are to blame for
my windswept monsoons,
You are to blame for
the love in the rain;
You are to blame for
the doubtlessness, the trust,
You are to blame for
erasing my despair & pain.
You are to blame for
making me feel beautiful,
You are to blame for
every unshed tear;
You are to blame for
the rainbows in my life,
You are to blame for
every dissolving fear.

Ц Ц Ц Ц

You are to blame for
the unending melody I hear,
You are to blame for
my love filled twilights;
You are to blame for
my getting addicted to you,
You are to blame for
my starlit and full moon nights.
You are to blame for
making me lose the fear of loss,
You are to blame for
finding the hidden feelings in me;
You are to blame for
discovering my dreams,
You are to blame for
the future with you that I see.

Ц Ц Ц Ц

You are to blame for my
warm & cozy winters,
You are to blame for my
colors of beautiful spring;
You are to blame for
the lazy, breezy summers,
You are to blame for
the joy the seasons bring.
You are to blame for all
the good things in my life,
You are to blame, for all
of them are because of you;
You are to blame for changing my
life into a beautiful place,
There will always be a special
place in my life for You.

– Suhasini
(10th December 09)

You are ..

You are the lilting melody
in every song I sing;
You are the hope that comes
with blossoming spring.
You are the life that smiles
forth with every sunray;
You are the fragrance in
every path..every way.
You are the naughty
twinkle in my eyes;
You are the gold in my
bright blue skies.
You are the raindrops
that touch me and tease;
You are the soft breeze
that sets me at ease.
You are the murmur
that whispers in my ear;

You are the soothing promise
that allays my fear.
You are the reason for my
bright starlit night;
You are the canvas that
covers all in my sight.
You are the crystal prism
that colours my life so;
You are the memory that
haunts me wherever I go.
You are the voice that
calls me back to earth,
You are the warmth..
the comfortable hearth.
You are the life.. that
kindles my hopes anew;
You are my world..it is
nothing at all without You.

– Suhasini
7th Dec 2009

Suhasini Ramakrishnan

You are..

You are the lilting, soft tune that
stays on my lips night & day,
You are that little sparkle in my eyes
that makes them seem bright;
You are the little naughtiness in my
smile that makes it happy,
You are like moonlight, that smiles
back at me in the hours of night.
You are like the warmth in the first
sunray that teases me awake,
You are the soft promise of reassurance
that, at times I miss so much;
You are my prism; You glisten through
my tears and color my life,
You are my anchor, when I hurt..it is
Your palm I reach out to touch.

෧ ෨ ෧ ෨ ෧ ෨

You are the one who makes my little
joys seem big and beautiful,
You are the one who makes me
laugh for no real reason at all;
You are the one who makes senseless
fun seem meaningful in my life,
You are the one I trust completely, to
hold my hand if I falter..if I fall.
You are the one who plays the fool,
yet seem so adorable in that act,
You are the one who is deep, Your
depth unfathomable..like the sea;
You are the one who makes me want
to do things..to make you smile,
You are the one who makes me realize
that there are more sides to me.

৯৶ ৽৶ ৯৶ ৽৶ ৯৶ ৽৶

You are a part of the lives of so many,
You touch so many hearts,
You are someone all say are close to,
yet no one does truly know;
You are somewhat of a welcome mystery
to all whose lives You are in,
You are an enigma..there are chambers
in You where no one can go.
You are someone I respect for all that
You are..and all that You will be,
You are someone I know I will remember
for more reasons than one;
You are that friend who reads me..&
says exactly what I need to hear,
You are the one I trust to be there..till
You know that need for You is done.

❧ ❧ ❧ ❧ ❧ ❧

You are simple at heart, yet Your heart
at times keep away simple joys,
You are the reason I often smile..yet..
that smile doesn't touch your eye ;
You are a precious friend, close to my
heart..yet sometimes.. are so far away,
You are so distant at times, and seem
unreachable no matter what I try.
You are forever a fond memory, in spite
of being so real when I see You,
You are still that nameless warm hope
I carry inside my dreams..my day;
You are that precious indelible mark, that
I will cherish each day in my life,
You are more precious to me than You
know..& it will always be that way.

– Suhasini
(7th Dec. 2012)

Printed in the United States
By Bookmasters